Sermon Outlines
on Key Bible Themes

Hyman Appelman

BAKER BOOK HOUSE
Grand Rapids, Michigan

First printing, April 1979
Second printing, May 1980
Third printing, August 1982
Fourth printing, September 1983
Fifth printing, September 1984
Sixth printing, December 1985

Printed in the United States of America

Contents

Sermon Outlines
on Key Bible Themes

The Christt of Revelation (Revelation 1:18)

    I. "I am He that liveth."
        A. His eternal necessary self-existence.
        B. His immutability.
        C. His most perfect and blessed life.
            1. The author and giver of life.
            2. The only source and fountain of pure adequate, permanent happiness to angels and men.
    II. "And was dead."
        A. The self-living one was dead.
        B. "The Prince of Life" was slain (Acts 3:15).
        C. "The Lord of glory" was crucified" (1 Cor. 2:8).
        D. For us and for our sins.
   III. "I am alive for evermore."
        A. The Man Christ Jesus is alive for evermore.
        B. He will die no more (Rom. 6:9).
        C. He is seated at the right hand of the Father.
        D. He lives to succor and to save believers, to condemn and punish His enemies.

Prayer (Psalm 65:2)

    I. A Glorious Fact.
    God hears prayer. This fact may be proved:
        A. From the nature of God. Infinite intelligence. Infinite kindness. Infinite resources.
        B. From the teachings of Scripture. "The effectual, fervent prayer . . . (James 5:16).
        C. From the life of Jesus Christ.
        D. From the experience of believers: Moses. Elijah. David. Hezekiah. Daniel. Peter. Paul. Moderns.
    II. A Precious Privilege.
    We may come unto God in prayer.
        A. It is a great privilege to be permitted to unburden our hearts to a Being of perfect wisdom and goodness and

sympathy. The mere telling of such experiences will afford relief.

    B. How much greater is the privilege when that Being has power to aid and bless. "In everything by prayer and supplication with thanksgiving, let your requests be made known unto God."

    C. It is a great privilege to engage in intercessory prayer.

III. An Inspiring Prospect.

"Unto Thee shall all flesh come."

All the weak and needy shall come to the infinite source of strength and blessing.

    1. There is a correlation between God's supply and man's need.

    2. Divinely appointed means are in operation for bringing needy men to the wealthy God.

    3. The Word of God invites the approach of all men to the Hearer of prayer.

IV. Conclusion.

    A. Appreciate the fact.

    B. Use the privilege.

    C. Have faith in the prospect.

    D. Seek to extend them to others. Announce it to others. Persuade them to avail themselves of it.

A Prisoner's Alarming Question (Luke 7:19)

Doubt is not sin. It may be occasioned by illness, inactivity, setbacks, lack of knowledge, etc.

The Basis for Our Assurance —

  I. The Testimony of Prophecy.

    A. The person who should come.

    1. David's son (Ps. 89:29; 110:1).

    2. Immanuel (Isa. 7:14).

    3. The Mighty God (Isa. 9:6).

    B. The purposes of His coming.

    1. To guide as a Prophet (Deut. 18:18).

    2. To govern as a King (Ps. 2:6).

    3. To save as a Redeemer (Isa. 35:4).

    4. To feed as a Shepherd (Isa. 40:11).

    5. To reward as a Judge (Isa. 40:10; 33:33).

    C. The proofs of His coming.

    1. Miracles (Isa. 29:18; 35:5, 6).

    2. Reception by poor (Isa. 8:14; 53:1; 2 Pet. 1:19).

II. The Testimony of a Person.
   A. The nature of this Person.
   B. The fulfillment of the purposes.
   C. The incompatability of any other Person to fit description.
III. The Testimony of Proof.
   A. Infinite wisdom could not make a mistake.
   B. Infinite truth cannot mislead.
   C. Others have been tried.
IV. The Testimony of a Program.
   A. Passion for Christ.
   B. Purity of life.
   C. Persistence of purpose.

The Religion of the Bible (Luke 24:44)

The religion of the Bible rests on a foundation of historical facts.

The Bible is a scientific book, if teaching science correctly is a mark of its being such a book.

The Bible is a standard book on jurisprudence, and its teachings are the basis of all civilized law.

The Bible is supreme in ethics.

The Bible contains the model form of government which is more or less copied by all modern constitutional governments of today.

The Bible is a standard work in literature.

The Bible is full of political and commercial wisdom.

The Bible's rules for personal and family life have, when followed, led to the highest and best results.

The Bible contains sound hygienic principles.

The Bible is the only book that leads to Christ, to God, to salvation, to glory.

Starting with God (Philippians 3:13, 14)

A New Year offers a New Start.

Only with God can there be a New Start.

God stands ready to Forgive the Past and Fortify the Present.
   I. Remembrance of the Past.
      Past favors of God. Of men.
      Past fears which never materialized.
      Past failures showing our dependence on God.

II. Recognition of the Possibilities.

Opportunities for growth in Christ and in the service of our fellow men.

Opposition we are sure to face — forewarned is forearmed.

Offers from God through Christ of the Holy Spirit — presence, guidance, wisdom, power, fruit.

III. Resolutions in the Present.

Not to be idly nor too quickly made.

Not those so easily broken.

Determination to put God first always.

To see dedication through regardless of cost.

To spend more time in seeking God's fullness.

The Cure of the Incurable (Mark 5:25-34)

The story of the woman with the issue of blood has in it some up-to-the-minute lessons.

1. Sin, a disease incurable by any human agency or remedy.
2. Hence, all self-effort in vanity, vexation, despair.
3. Just where man comes to the end of self, he finds the beginning of God. (Cf. The Prodigal, Luke 15.) Man's extremity, God's opportunity.
4. Condition of healing. Voluntary appropriation of power in God. Virtue, not in faith, but in Christ. Specific act — laying hold of promise of God.
5. Cure. Immediate, complete, permanent, and often conscious.
6. Confession should follow, as duty, privilege; both honoring Christ and benefiting men. Her act had no precedent, but set one and became such (Matt. 14:36).
7. Further blessing follow, when full duty done (Rom. 10:9-10). Confession and salvation. Note "daughter" the word used by Christ after her confession.

Men's physicians are: Self-reformation; human resolve; new environment; association; the best environment did not help even Judas. Education changes and heals forms of sin, but not the root. Ritualism; intoxication; gaiety; pleasure; comparison with others for self-justification; infidelity; wreck of faith.

The "touch" needed; not historic, scholastic, aesthetic, ethic, or ecclesiastic, but divine.

The Two Rabbis (John 3:1-4)

I. The Teacher Come from God.

A. Accessible to men (Vs. 1, 2; Matt. 8:34; 9:28; 11:28; 15:1; Mark 1:8; John 4:40).
B. Commissioned of God (Vs. 2; Deut. 18:18; John 8: 28; John 12:49; John 14:10; John 18:8; Heb. 1:1, 2).
C. Confirmed by miracles (Vs. 2; Luke 23:47; John 2:11; John 9:33; John 10:38; John 14:11; Acts 2:22).

II. A Teacher Able to Teach.
A. Of the new birth (Vs. 3; John 1:13; II Cor. 5:17; Gal. 6:15; James 1:18; I Peter 1:23; I John 3:9).
B. Of the Spirit's Power (Vs. 6; John 14:26; John 16:13; Rom. 8:14; I Cor. 1:22; Titus 3:5).
C. Of the heavenly things (Vs. 12; John 6:33; John 6:51; John 14:3; John 16:28; I Cor. 15:47; I Thess. 4:16).

III. A Teacher Able to Save.
A. Lifted up to save (Vs. 14; Num. 21:9; John 8:28; John 12:32; I Cor. 2:2; Gal. 6:15; I John 1:7).
B. Exalted to Save (Acts 2:36; 3:19; Phil. 2:9-11).
C. Enthroned to save (Heb. 7:25; Jude 23, 24; I Peter 1:3-5).

The Lamb of God

Forgiveness of sins through the atoning sacrifice of Christ, is a blessing which it is the glory of God to reveal, and the privilege of Christians to experience.

I. Sin, which is the transgression of the law, justly exposes the offender to the punishment of death.
II. A gracious God, though justly offended by the sins of men, has in mercy made provision for the restoration of all who repent and believe.
III. To the faith of believers divine provision was exhibited in the types and prophecies in the Old Testament.
IV. All these types and prophecies were fulfilled by the atoning death and triumphant resurrection of our Lord.
V. Through the sacrifice and resurrection of Christ, sinners of all conditions are entitled to the blessings of redemption.

Consider:
1. The influence of these truths upon the mind (Rom. 5:1-5).
2. The encouragement hereby given to the returning sinner.
3. The madness of expecting salvation in any other way.

The Resurrection of Jesus

Sin is described in Scripture as a deadly plague, as poison, as a crime against nature. It is man's worst enemy. It is treason against God. By its nature, effects, its manward and Godward work, it deserves death. It is a capital crime.

The redemptive work of Christ is thus described by Paul: "Whom God hath set forth to be a propitiation through faith in his blood, to declare his righteousness for the remission of sins that are past through the forbearance of God; To declare, I say, at this time his righteousness: that he might be just, and the justifier of him which believeth in Jesus" (Romans 3:25, 26).

It was not that God had to be made willing to receive sinful man, but that it had to be made right for Him to do so.

The act of righteousness by which Christ secured for the world this state of grace was His death.

The death of Christ brought the world into salvable relations to God.

The great proof the disciples advanced to the world for the truth of their message was the resurrection of Christ.

Among the evidences of the resurrection are the many predictions of the Scriptures and of Jesus Himself that He would rise from the dead.

The testimony of the Jews and the Roman soldiers who watched the sepulchre is not the least valuable as to the resurrection of Jesus.

1. The Resurrection of Jesus was a complete verification of all His claims for Himself.

2. The Resurrection of Jesus was God's witness to His finished and perfect work.

3. The Resurrection of Jesus is God's warning to the world that there will be the Day of Judgment. "And the times of this ignorance God winked at; but now commandeth all men everywhere to repent: Because he hath appointed a day, in the which he will judge the world in righteousness by that man whom he hath ordained; whereof he hath given assurance unto all men, in that he hath raised him from the dead" (Acts 17:30, 31).

4. The Resurrection of Jesus is the one great proof of the hereafter and all its glories and terrors.

Christ in His Earthly Life (Philippians 2:5-11)

Types representing Christ:

Adam — as the head of the human race.

Melchizedek — of the priesthood of Christ.
Moses with Joshua — of the prophetic office.
David with Solomon — of His Kingship.
Israel as a nation, a type of Christ.

To Abraham the coming Christ was the longed-for Seed; to Jacob, a Deliverer; to Moses, a revelation of glory; to David, an Heir.

There was a great assembly in heaven. Christ made Himself responsible, personally, for the sin and state of man.

He rises like a monarch, relinquishing royal power and office for a time, lays aside His crown and robes, and descends from the throne. "He emptied Himself of His divine glory, and laid His divine attributes, omnipotence, omniscience, omnipresence, under temporary, voluntary limitations."

Christ's humanity is seen in His humiliation, divinity in His exaltation. He entered the lowest condition of man — "lying in the manger" — for even savages have better accommodations.

Jesus was in constant communication with His Father. The unseen world was constantly open to His vision.

Three divine manifestations follow His baptism.

The Open Heaven was the attestation of God to His sinlessness.

The Voice of God was the open acknowledgment of His Sonship.

The Descending Spirit was the anointing which gave Him His name — the Christ. It was God's strength given to Jesus, the setting apart of Jesus to His life work, anointing Him with power for service, the preparation for temptation.

The work of Jesus was threefold. He saved bodies, souls, and spirits. His was a mission to sickness, sorrow and sin. He contemplated the whole man.

Jesus came as a witness for God. He came to reveal God to man.

Jesus also revealed God in man.

The great revelation was the revelation of the will of God.

Jesus was Himself a revelation of God — "God manifest in the flesh."

It was not devotion to man first of all, but to God, which produced that perfect self-abnegation which showed itself in the self-forgetfulness and self-sacrifice of Jesus.

In Christ there is the proclamation of the three forms of peace — peace from God, peace with God, and the peace of God.

The peace of God covers peace for the past with all its sins and mistakes; peace for the present with all its anxieties and burdens; and peace for the future, with all its hopes and fears down to the end into eternity.

Renan, who denied the divinity of Jesus as Christians accept it, writes as follows: "The incomparable man to whom the universal conscience has decreed the title of Son of God, and that with justice. Repose now in Thy glory, noble founder! Thy work is finished; Thy divinity is established . . . a thousand times more alive, a thousand times more beloved, since Thy death than during Thy passage here below, Thou shalt become the cornerstone of humanity so entirely that to tear Thy name from this world would be to rend it to its foundation. Between Thee and God there will be no longer any distinction."

The Unitarian, Theodore Parker, wrote: "Shall we be told such a man never lived? The whole story is a lie? Suppose that Plato or Newton never lived: who did their works and thought their thoughts? It takes a Newton to forge a Newton. What man could have fabricated Jesus? None but a Jesus."

Jean Paul Richter thus writes of Jesus: "The holiest among the mighty, the mightiest among the holy, lifted with His pierced hands empires off their hinges, and turned the stream of centuries out of its channel and still governs the ages."

The Effects of Piety on a Nation (Genesis 18:32)

    I. Who are the Pious Men?
       Separated from surrounding wickedness.
       Firmly attached to the doctrines of God.
       Cultivate cordial, brotherly love.
       Zealously endeavoring to spread of the gospel.

    II. The effects which we are warranted to expect such conduct to insure.
       Sodom would have been spared.
       God preserves nations for the sake of pious men.
       Let pious men prevail, and they will keep up the freedom of a land.
       Spiritual benefits will be secured.

    III. You must be pious yourself.

The Father and Jesus (John 5:26)

    I. Jesus possessed a unique relationship to the Father (John 10:30; 8:58; 14:9).

II. He maintained an unbroken fellowship with the Father (John 5:17; 9:4; 15:10).

III. By the New Birth we become "partakers of the divine nature" (II Peter 1:4; I John 3:9; Heb. 12:10).

Calvary

Calvary is surely the most sacred place on the face of the earth. In the geography of the soul it has no rival. Its voices are authoritative, revealing, searching, comforting, and inspiring. It is the Holy of Holies of the Holy Land, because the place where Jesus died, "the Just for the unjust, that He might bring us to God."

I. Calvary Is the Weeping Place of Penitence.

Zechariah 12:10; Luke 22:33-48. It is the Christian's place of weeping, deepen our sense of need, make more vivid our consciousness and hatred of sin, give us a keener appraisment of the value of pardon, make more real our joy in the realization of full salvation.

II. Calvary Is the Resting Place of Faith.

Galatians 2:20. "All my theology is contained in four little words, 'Christ died for me.'"

III. Calvary Is the Birthplace of Love.

"We love Him because He first loved us." Of our love for Christ, and for one another.

IV. Calvary Is the Hiding Place from Judgment.
   Its Certainty.
   Its Thoroughness.
   Its Purpose.

> Ah! Show me that happiest place,
> The place of Thy people's abode,
> Where saints in an ecstasy gaze,
> And hang on a crucified God;
> Thy love for a sinner declare,
> Thy passion and death on the tree;
> My spirit to Calvary bear,
> To suffer and triumph with Thee.

We are not to love the world —

Because it is impossible to love the world and to love God at one and the same time.

Because the world and all for which it stands is passing away.

Because it is only he that doeth the will of God that abideth forever.

The Handwriting on the Wall (Daniel 5)

   I. Belshazzar learned nothing from Nebuchadnezzar's fall.
  II. Belshazzar had not humbled himself before the Lord.
 III. He had seen Nebuchadnezzar's fate, but he had not learned humility.
 IV. He was guilty of the pride of self-sufficiency.
  V. He had profaned sacred things. For us: Sunday; Bible; Conscience.

Going God's Way (Isaiah 30:21)

   I. There must be a surrendered will.
  II. A studying mind.
 III. A walking faith.

Choosing Life (Deuteronomy 30:19-20)

   I. By loving your God.
  II. By obeying His voice.
 III. By holding fast to Him.

On Being Mature (Philippians 3:12-15)

Ours is an age seeking maturity. Paul gives the steps leading to Christian Maturity.

   I. Recognizing Our Limitations.
     A. 1. Paul recognized his *need*.
        2. Recognized his shortcomings.
     B. 1. To have a vital Christian experience we must recognize our own needs.
        2. There must be a diagnosis before we can be healthy.
        3. Recognition of need comes before repentance.
     C. 1. We must evaluate our limitations.
        2. Tragedy to do more than we can do adequately.
  II. Forgetting Our Failures.
     A. Paul.
        1. Persecution of the Christians.
        2. Religion of legalism.
     B. We.
        1. Not dwelling on past mistakes.
        2. Essence.

Horeb — Mount of Contrasts (I Kings 19:11)

I. The WIND is a symbol of the elusive, expansive force of the SPIRIT.
> (The only bad weather is stagnant weather.)

II. The EARTHQUAKE is a symbol of the aggressive force of the SPIRIT.
> (Such a thing as fatal rigidity.)

III. The FIRE is the symbol of the intensive force of the SPIRIT.

IV. The VOICE is the symbol of the personal influence of the SPIRIT.

Lowering the Sea (II Kings 16:17)

We have not lowered the Sea.
But we have frustrated the Divine Plan.
Maimed good and useful things.
Undone the religious work of the past.
Treated sacred things irreverently.
Sinned through craven fear.
Caused others to sin.
Broken the Commandments of God.

Rediscovering the Bible (II Kings 23:2)

Bethlehem and the Bible are organically related.
The Bible is the manger in which Christ is laid.
Not a rediscovered building but a rediscovered book.
This supplied the dynamic for a religious revival.
By rediscovering the Bible Josiah rediscovered God.

Jabez' Prayer (I Chronicles 4:10)

It was a prayer for personal benediction.
For practical extension.
For providential direction.
For perpetual protection.

Joseph's Vision (Genesis 41:38)

I. A Fact about His Brothers — They despised his dreams (Gen. 37:34).

II. A Fact about Potiphar's Wife — She misrepresented his morals (Gen. 39:9).

III. A Fact about the Butler — He forgot his favor (Gen. 40: 14, 15).

IV. A Fact about Joseph — He refused to retaliate (Gen. 50: 16, 17).

David's Sin (II Samuel 11-12)

I. The Cause (II Sam. 11:1).

II. The Course.
  He saw a woman bathing.
  He sent and inquired concerning the woman.
  He sent messengers and took her.
  He caused the death of Uriah.

III. The Curse.
  "Who sows the serpent's teeth must not hope to reap a joyous harvest."
  Nathan pronounced the curse of God (II Sam. 12:10-12).

IV. The Cure (Ps. 32:3-4; 32:5; Ps. 51).
  Full confession of sin.
  David was conscious of sin because he was conscious of God's holiness.

The Ordeal of a Man's Faith (Genesis 22:1)

I. The Testing of Abraham's Faith.

II. The Testimony of Abraham's Faith— his obedience.

III. The Triumph of Abraham's Faith — God takes control.

Summary of Bible (Romans 6:23)

I. What is not said.

II. What is said.

III. To whom is it said.

IV. Why is it said.

Abraham's Faith (Genesis 12:1-2)

I. The Call to Go.

V/C 8/16/20

16

II. The Call to Grow (Gen. 12:8).
III. The Call to Give.
   To Give In (Gen. 13:10-11).
   To Give Out (Gen. 14:23).
   To Give Up (Gen. 22:2).

The Unshaken Riches (II Timothy 1:12; Romans 8:28.

"The wicked are like the troubled seas which cannot rest"
(Isaiah 57:20).
   I. Christian Experience (Dr. James Simpson, Edinburgh,
      saying: "Of this I am sure, that Jesus Christ is my Sav-
      iour.")
  II. Divine Providence (Napoleon saying to Queen Maria
      Theresa, Austria: "God is on the side of the big bat-
      talions," then being defeated at the age of forty-six,
      despite his big battalions.)
 III. The Assurance of the Immortal Life (Child dying, saying
      to his father: "Good night, father, I shall see you in
      the morning.")
      (Bishop of London trying to comfort child in the hour
      of death, saying to the child, "Would you be afraid if
      I carried you into the next room?")

The Sound of Marching (II Samuel 5:24)

This warning sign, this harbinger of revival was heard only
by those in the battle, the right men in the right place at the
right time.

(General Booth, to his eldest daughter, "the Marechale," when
much discouraged during the early days of her work in Paris,
advised her to keep her eyes off the waves and fix them on the
tide.)
   I. A Spirit of Lawlessness in the World and Deadness in the
      Church (Ps. 119:126).
      Not an indication that revival is impossible, but that it is
      imperative.
  II. A Spirit of Dissatisfaction (Spiritual Restlessness).
      Thirst for God (Ps. 42:1).
         For the holiness of God.
         For the power of God (Ps. 42:3).

17

For the manifestation of God (Ps. 63:1).
For the truth of God.

III. A Spirit of Sin-consciousness (Isa. 57:15; James 5:16).

IV. A Spirit of Tender Concern (Ps. 102:13, 14; Jer. 9:1).

V. A Spirit of Expectancy.
"If God has done it there, may He not do it here also" (Isa. 43:13).

VI. A Spirit of Unity.
Sectarianism — Exclusivism — Attitude of Spiritual Superiority (Ps. 133).

VII. A Spirit of Prayer (Hos. 10:12).
"Satan laughs at our toil, mocks at our wisdom, but trembles when we pray."

The Time Is Now (Romans 13:11)

Redeem the time now.

I. The Love of Christ Constrains Us (II Cor. 5:14).

II. The Lost Souls of Men Call Us (I Cor. 15:34).

III. The Lack of Time Compels Us (Rom. 13:11).

"Say not ye, There are yet four months, and then cometh harvest? behold, I say unto you, Lift up your eyes, and look on the fields; for they are white already to harvest" (John 4:35).

> Lift up our eyes and look,
> Lift up our hearts and pray,
> Lift up our hands and give,
> Lift up our feet and go.

A Lost Christ (Luke 2:41-49)

The most unlikely person is the first to lose Him — His mother.
You may get very close to Jesus and you may lose Him.
Some of you may not understand.
Some of you will understand because you saw Him once — a church member, an official, a Christian worker, a preacher (Samson a whole church = rich, etc., "poor, wretched, ignorant.")
She lost Him in the most unlikely place.
Where people generally go to find Him.
Not in theater. Not getting drunk. Not in any extravagant vice. Not with giddy multitude.
You may be best and lose Him.

"Supposing He was in the company"
   What is the use of supposing?
   It is the real thing we need.
   It is Jesus we need.
   All else is empty without Him.
   All else is useless without Him.
HAVE you lost Him?
   Is Jesus as dear to you . . . ?
   Are you as enthused — Bible — prayer?
   You should have grown.
   Have you drifted? Cold?
   Have you any real, unbroken fellowship with Him?
   God sends this message to call a halt.
SHE found Him where she lost Him — had to tramp back four
      days.
   The Prodigal Son found his father in the old homestead.
   No such thing as dodging Him.
ARE you willing to find Christ?
   Will you seek Him tonight?
   Your soul is prompting you.
   Your conscience is prompting you.
   The Holy Spirit is prompting you.
   (Lady on platform stood but did not come. Preacher offered
      to pray there. No, she did it publicly.)

Death of Christ, For Whom (Romans 5:6)

   I. The kind of people for whom Christ died — "the ungod-
      ly."
   II. The cause of His death — "for our sins" (I Cor. 15:3).
   III. The setting of His death — "according to Scriptures" (I
      Cor. 15:3).
   IV. The reach of His death — "for all."
   V. The merits of His death.

Ministry, God's Gifts (Ephesians 4:11-13)

   I. Its Institution.
   II. Its Duration.
            Has to do with eternity.
            With the inner man.
            Every speaking witness of man's feebleness and of
               God's strength.

Mainly with the conscience of men. It is not the intellect, then, but the conscience, not the imagination, but the conscience, not the passions, but the conscience — to which the minister is to commend himself in the sight of God.

III. Its Implication.
Courage.
Tenderness.
Perseverance.

Grace — Measure of (Ephesians 2:8)

I. The Meaning of Grace.
Defies defining.
Illimitable.
Infinite.
Illustrated but never defined.
The reforming mercy of God without regard to merit.

II. The Method of Grace (Gal. 1:4).

III. The Message of Grace.
Forgiveness of sins.
Restoration.
Sanctification.

More than Conquerors (Romans 8:37) 5/20/18

I. The certainty of victory.
"We are more than conquerors."

II. The spirit of victory.
"In all these things."

III. The secret of victory.
Nothing could separate Paul from the love of Christ.

Working Faith (Mark 9:23)

What will Faith do for you.

I. Preserve your freedom.

II. Answer principal problems of your life — Why? Whence? Whither?

III. Enlarge your knowledge.

IV. Preserve your quality.

V. Enable you to possess the "mind of Christ."

Salvation, from Without (Acts 16:31)

Who can remake you?
Why must salvation come from without?

I. Because human nature has contracted a bigger debt than it can pay.
II. Because you can destroy life, but you cannot create it.
III. We need a teacher for our minds, a physician for our bodies, and a Redeemer for our souls — a Redeemer from without — outside of humanity with its weaknesses, its sins and its rebellion.
IV. Because no man can lift himself by his boot-straps.

The Virgin-born Christ (Galatians 4:4)

I. The Holy Spirit created a perfectly new human nature in the womb of Mary, a new Adam, a new Creature, a new Pattern.
II. God had been in nature as Providence.
III. He had been in history as Prophecy.
IV. Now, when the fullness of time is come, God appears in history as a Man.

God's Love (I John 4:10)

I. God does not love us because He needs us.
II. He loves us because He has put some of His love in us.
III. God does not love us because we are valuable.
IV. We are valuable because He loves us.

Why I Am a Soul-winner (Matthew 9:35 ff.)

I. Because Jesus Was.
II. Harvest Is So Great.
III. Laborers Are So Few.
IV. Of the Great Commission.
V. The Unfulfilled Prophecies Concerning Christ's Return.
VI. I Don't Want the Blood of Sinners on My Hands.
VII. Of What I've Experienced.

Why Win the Jews

    I. Jesus Reveals Man to Himself.

   II. Man's Everyday Life Is Sacredly Significant.

  III. Man's Worship Determines His Sense of Worth.

  IV. Life at Its Best Is Not Good Enough.

   V. Life in Ruins Can Be Remade.

The Source of Salvation: The Cross of Christ (John 19:18)

    I. Human Depravity Revealed by Christ's Moral Grandeur.

   II. The Christian's Inadequacy Disclosed at Testing Time.

  III. World's Judgment Untrustworthy Concerning Christ.

  IV. Mental Agony of Christ's Experience.

   V. Incalculable Suffering of the Crucifixion.

  VI. Desolation of Soul When Christ became Sin.

 VII. Saving Power of the Cross.

VIII. Cross a Way of Life.

The Master Motive: The Lordship of Christ (John 20:28)

    I. Master Motive in the Hierarchy of Motives — Partnership with the Living Lord.

   II. Power That Can Turn Despair into Hope.

  III. Conviction That Leads to Unreserved Committal.

  IV. Companionship That Blesses All of Life.

   V. Love That Fulfills the Law of Christ.

  VI. Experience That Testifies to Saving Truth.

"Occupy Till I Come" (Luke 19:13)   *V/C 2023*

    I. The Goal We Hold in View.
       Personal — Church — Community — Souls.

   II. The Obstacles — Opposition We Face.
       Satan — Weakness of Flesh — Attitudes of Those Trying to Win.

  III. Allies We May Count On.
       Holy Spirit — Bible — Prayer — Other Christians.

  IV. Victories We Can Anticipate.
       Personal — Others — Souls.

Terror of the Lord.
    Universal — Inescapable — Irreversible — Irreducible.
Testing of the Gospel.
    Authenticity — Adaptability — Availability.
Triumph of Christian.
    Personal Assurance — Entrusted Cares — Assured Outcome.

Source of Salvation: Cross of Christ

  I. Battlefield.
 II. Altar.
III. Meeting Place.
IV. Pulpit.
 V. Judgment Bar.

Three Times in a Nation's History (Luke 19:41-44)

  I. A Day of Grace.
Today.
Presence of Christ.
Pleadings of Holy Spirit, "this thy day."
 II. A Day of Blindness, "hid from thine eyes."
Ignorance (Spiritual).
Inattentiveness (preoccupation).
Indifference (soul vs. self vs. sin).
III. A Day of Judgment, "thine enemies . . . another. . . ."
Temporal (here and now).
Involving (others).
Eternal (Hell).

God's Description of His Son (Isaiah 42:1-4)

Isaiah the evangelist of Old Testament.
The John the Baptist of Old Testament.
  I. The Character of the Messiah.
    A. God's servant (Phil. 2:5-11).
    B. God's elect chosen for task.
 II. The Qualifications of the Messiah.
    A. God put His Spirit upon Christ as a public recognition of His Messiahship.

B. To fortify Him against the attacks of Satan.

C. To annoint Him for preaching the gospel.

D. For the purpose of working miracles.

III. The Conquests of the Messiah.

    A. Unostentatiously — not as world.

    B. Tenderly and compassionately.

    C. Courageously and fearlessly, never more discouragements.

    D. We are discouraged by the doubtful issue of our undertaking.

      1. By the impotency of our powers.

      2. By the magnitude of the opposition raised against us.

IV. The Claims of the Messiah.

    A. Read of Him.

    B. Study His character.

    C. Believe on His Name.

    D. Obey His behests.

Three Similitudes

I. The Stung Israelite and the Guilty Sinner.

    A. As the Israelite had death in his bosom, so the sinner (Heb. 2:14). Although the latter sting may not be felt as was the former.

    B. The Israelite wanted all means of cure, and had not God appointed the serpent, he had perished.

    C. As helpless is the sinner until God shows us His Christ.

II. The Brazen Serpent and Christ.

    A. The serpent was accursed of God. Christ was made accursed for us.

    B. The brazen serpent had the likeness of the serpent, but not the poison. Christ came in the similitude of sinful flesh, without sin.

    C. The brazen serpent was uplifted on a pole; Christ on the cross.

    D. As the poison of the serpent was healed by a serpent; so the sin of man by Man. (Rom. 5:1; I Cor. 15:21). But Christ had power in Himself to heal us which the other had not.

    E. The brazen serpent was not the device of an Israelite, but of God; so no man could have found out such a means of salvation as that established by Christ.

III. The Israelites Looking on the Serpent and the Sinners Believing in Christ.
   A. The Israelite was healed only by looking; so the sinner is justified only by believing.
   B. As looking, as well as the rest of the senses, is a passion rather than an action; so in justification thou art a patient rather than an agent; thou holdest thy beggars hands to receive, that is all.
   C. The Israelites before they looked up to the brazen serpent for help —
      1. Felt themselves stung.
      2. Believed that God would heal them by that serpent. So the sinner must —
      1. Feel himself a sinner, be burdened and heavy laden (Matt. 11:28) before he will or can come to Christ. A man that feels not himself sick, seeks not a physician.
      2. He must believe that in Christ there is all-sufficient help.
   D. The stung Israelite looked on the serpent with a pitiful, humble, craving, wishful eye. Weeping also for the very pain of his sting; with such an eye that the believing sinner doth look on Christ crucified (Zech. 12:10).
   E. The Israelite by looking on the brazen serpent, received ease presently, and was rid of the poison and of the living serpent, and so therein was made, like the brazen serpent, void of all poison. So the believer by looking on Christ, is eased of his guilty, accusing conscience (Rom. 5:1) and is transformed into the image of Christ (II Cor. 3:18).
   F. Even the squint-eyed or purblind Israelite was healed; so the weak believer, being a true believer, is healed by Christ.
   G. Though the Israelite was stung every so often, yet if he looked up to the serpent he was healed. As we are daily stung by sin, so we must daily look up to Christ crucified. Every new sin must have a fresh act of faith and repentance. Yet there are two differences between their looking on the serpent and our looking by faith on Christ.
      1. By looking they lived, but yet so after that they died: But here by believing in Christ, we gain an eternal life.

2. They looked on the serpent, but the serpent could not look on them; but here, as thou lookest on Christ, so He on thee, as once on Peter, and on Mary, and on John, from the cross, and thy comfort must rather be in Christ's looking on thee, than in thy looking on Him.

Faith for Salvation

When Oliver Cromwell was dying he told his weeping wife and children what his hope and treasures were. Think of the treasures the Lord Protector of England might have amassed to hand down to his family. What did he actually leave them?

"My children," he said, "I leave you the Covenant to feed upon."

Was that all? That was all. But was it not enough? It was his own chief treasure. For as he lay facing the eternal world, at the hour when falsities are torn from our eyes, he said: "It is holy and true. It is holy and true. It is holy and true! Who made it holy and true? The Mediator of the Covenant!" And at another time: "The Covenant is but one: faith in the Covenant is my only support; and if I believe not, He abides faithful."

On which Carlyle ejaculates: "Yea, my brave one; even so! The Covenant, and eternal soul of Covenants, remains sure to all the faithful: deeper than the foundations of the world; earlier than they, and more lasting than they!" It was Cromwell's faith in God's pledged support that made him strong to stand for truth and liberty against the forces of this world, and his faith bore the test of events. His Covenant God proved Himself true.

Crusade. "God Wills It."

A Careful Diagnosis.
    Not the skin rash but what causes it.
    Fear.
    Escape mechanisms.
    Shallow religion.
An Intelligent Prescription.
    Not criticism.
    Not isolationism.
    Substitutions.
    How other generations met it.

What has worked in the past.
The preaching of the gospel.
An Earnest Application.
The Jihad of the Muslims.
A Christian crusade.
Starting with pastors.
Christian cells.
Attack.

Preach the Gospel

The gospel is a fact: therefore, tell it simply.
It is an entrusted fact: therefore, tell it cheerily.
It is a fact of infinite moment: therefore, tell it earnestly.
It is a fact of infinite love: therefore, tell it pathetically.
It is a fact difficult of comprehension to many: therefore, tell it with illustration.
It is a fact about a person: therefore, preach Christ.

Caleb (Joshua 14:8)

I. A Man for the Times.
II. "Dog" or "All Heart."
III. His Faithful Following of His God.
    1. Universally without dividing.
    2. Fully and sincerely, without dissembling.
    3. Wholly and cheerfully without disputing.
    4. Constantly without declining.
IV. His Favored Portion.
    1. His life preserved in the hour of judgment.
    2. Comforted with a long life of vigor.
    3. Received great honor among his brethren.
    4. Distinguished by being put upon the hardest service.
    5. Enjoyed what he had once seen.
    6. Left a blessing for his children.

Redemption (Psalm 49:8)

I. Subject — soul.
    A. Its powers — knowledge and choice.
    B. Its affections — God or sin.
    C. Its duration — forever.

II. The Price of the Redemption Is Vast, Precious.

III. The Period of Its Accomplishment Is Limited.

Three Wells (Isaiah 12:3)

1. God's love.
2. Christ's blood.
3. Spirit's power.

The Way to Heaven (Isaiah 35:8-10)

1. It is a highway.
2. It is a holy way.
3. It is a safe way.
4. It is a plain way.
5. It is a happy way.
6. It is a raised way.
7. It is a simple way.

Seeking (Isaiah 55:7-12)

1. Seek the knowledge of the Lord (John 1:18; Eph. 1:17; II Cor. 4:8; I John 5:20; Matt. 11:27).
2. Seek His favor — His image (Eph. 4:22-24).
3. Seek Communion with Him (Eph. 4:18; Col. 1:21; II Cor. 6:16; John 14:23; Eph. 2:21, 22; I John 1:3).
4. The everlasting vision and enjoyment of Him (Matt. 5:8; I John 3:2; Rev. 21:3-7; 22:3-4).

The Sinner (Zechariah 3)

1. The danger he is in.
2. We must warn him.
3. The need for haste.
4. How to warn him.

God's Messenger Foretold (Malachi 3)

1. He taught by pithy, pointed sayings.
2. He taught by examples (Matt. 5:20).
3. He taught by action (took a child in His arms).
4. He taught by parable.

Consider This Jesus As the Saviour

1. Jesus the matchless Son of God.
2. Jesus of Bethlehem's manger.
3. Jesus of Galilee's works.
4. Jesus of Gethsemane's blood sweat.
5. Jesus of Calvary's despised death.
6. Jesus of Heaven's intercessory throne.

The Forgiveness of Sin (Matthew 9:2-8)

The world's first need is forgiveness of sin.
Christ has divine authority to forgive sins.
Christ's mission on earth brings the forgiveness of sins.
By His incarnation.
Through His atonement.
In His present power.

The Commission of Service. "Go quickly . . ." (Matthew 28:7)

1. It is Christ's part — dying for our sins.
2. It is God's part — raising Christ from the dead.
3. It is our part — evangelize a lost world.

The only hope for the lost world is Golgotha's cross and Joseph's empty tomb.

The Lord's Power (Mark 5:36)

The Lord had power over devils, disease, death, incurable cases.

1. Do not be afraid that your sins are too many.
2. Do not be afraid that His love is too shallow.
3. Do not be afraid that the word of God will fail.
4. Only believe that He is able to save.
5. Only believe that He is willing to save.
6. Only believe that He does save.
7. Only believe that He has saved.

The Way (John 14:1, 4)

1. He is the way of peace (Luke 1:79; Eph. 2:14).
2. He is the way of life (Prov. 15:24; Col. 3:4).
3. He is the way of holiness (Isa. 35:8; I Cor. 1:30).
4. He is the one way (Jer. 32:39; 10:1; Acts 4:12).

Love

1. It will keep us very near to Jesus.
2. It is the secret of success as a Christian.
3. It is entrusted with the gravest responsibilities (John 19: 26, 27).
4. It has wonderful discernment (John 21:7).
5. It follows willingly (Ruth).

The Church Today (Acts 2:1-5) *Done*

1. The church in the beginning was simply a body of believers waiting on their knees for God.
2. God is longing to see the church once more upon her knees.
3. We must connect our modern church work once more with divine power.
4. Life begins at the cross, but service begins at Pentecost.
5. A pure gospel.
6. United prayers.

A Great Theme (II Corinthians 2:2)

1. Redemption is by Christ crucified (Eph. 1:7; I Peter 1: 10; Gal. 3:13; Col. 1:14; Rev. 5:9).
2. Peace of conscience comes through Christ crucified (Col. 1:20).
3. Death to sin comes through Christ crucified (Gal. 2:20; 6:14).
4. The supreme argument of life is Christ crucified (Eph. 5:2).
5. The supreme example of patience is in Christ crucified (I Peter 2:20-24).
6. Enmity to His cross is a fatal sin (Heb. 10:29; Phil. 2: 18, 19).
7. Our King to communicate holiness—pouring out His Spirit.
   a. Ruling in our hearts.
   b. Giving us dominion over sin.
   c. Our final deliverer from all evil.

A Memorial (I Corinthians 11:24)

I. A Memorial of the Past.
II. A Symbol for the Present.
III. A Prophecy for the Future.

Faith

1. Faith is dependence on God — regardless.
   a. Moses at the Red Sea.
   b. Joshua at Jericho.
   c. Paul and Silas in jail.
   d. Luther at Worms.
   e. Wesley and Whitefield.
2. Faith comes by study of God's Word (Rom. 10:17).
3. Faith comes by study of men in faith.
4. Faith comes by personal testing and tested experiences.
5. Faith leads to holiness of self-denying living.
6. Faith leads to much secret prayer.
7. Faith leads to enduring, persistent, intensive effort.
8. Faith drives.
9. Faith goes.
10. Faith works.

Four Great Things (Titus 2)

I. A Great Revelation (vs. 11).
II. A Great Obligation (vs. 12).
III. A Great Inspiration (vs. 13).
IV. A Great Salvation (vs. 14).

Gospel Salvation Is Great (Hebrews 3)

1. The author of this salvation (Isa. 9:6; I Tim. 3:16; Isa. 59:16).
2. The means (Rom. 8:3; Isa. 53:3; Heb. 9:22).
3. The salvation itself.
   a. Saved from the guilt of all our sins (Rom. 8:1; Acts 13:39).
   b. Saved from the power of sin (Rom. 6:6, 14).
   c. Saved from the contagion of sin (I John 3:9; Ezek. 36: 25, 29).
   d. Saved from fear (I John 4:18; I Cor. 15:55; Isa. 12:11).
   e. Saved from the power of the grave (I Cor. 15:53; Phil. 3:21).
   f. Saved from hell and all misery (Rev. 7:17; Ps. 16:11).

The Blood That Speaks of Sin (Exodus 12:24)

I. Of Sacrifice — Lamb slain.

II. Of Satisfaction — Purpose of God accomplished through it.
III. Of Substitution — Lamb slain for house: Christ for us.
IV. Of Submission — Sprinkled blood spoke of faith and obedience of the household.
V. Of Salvation — Their safety depended on blood.

Faith (Hebrews 11)

The believer like David has five pebbles available.
1. God is.
2. God has.
3. God does.
4. God can.
5. God will.

The Secret Faith (Hebrews 11)

How faith accomplishes such results:
1. Faith is convinced that God exists.
2. Faith is convinced that God is capable of bestowing.
3. Faith is convinced that God is blessing (vs. 6).
4. Faith is convinced that God is faithful (vs. 11).
5. Faith is convinced that God is able (vs. 19).
6. Faith is convinced that God is with His people (vs. 27).

The Power of Faith (Hebrews 11)

What it does for men.
The Christian is called to be — to do — to endure — to suffer.

Helps to Prevailing Prayer (James 5)

I. Earnestness (James 5:16).
II. Perseverance (Luke 18:4-8).
III. Union for One Object (Matt. 18:19).
IV. Fasting (Matt. 17:21).
V. Large Requests (Ps. 81:10).
VI. Submission (Matt. 26:39).

Christ's Blood Cleanses (I John 1:7)

I. The Disease — sin.
II. The Remedy — blood of Jesus.
III. The Result — cleansing.
IV. The Condition — I John 1:9.